JESUS OUR JOY

Christian Focus Publications publishes biblically-accurate books for adults and children. The books in the adult range are published in three imprints.

Christian Heritage contains classic writings from the past.

Christian Focus contains popular works including biographies, commentaries, doctrine, and Christian living.

Mentor focuses on books written at a level suitable for Bible College and seminary students, pastors, and others; the imprint includes commentaries, doctrinal studies, examination of current issues, and church history.

For a free catalogue of all our titles,
please write to
Christian Focus Publications,
Geanies House, Fearn,
Ross-shire, IV20 1TW, Great Britain

For details of our titles visit us on our web site
http://www.christianfocus.com

Learning about True Spirituality

JESUS
OUR JOY

Wallace Benn

Christian Focus

For my colleagues
in
CHICHESTER DIOCESE
with
grateful thanks.

Contents

ISBN 1 85792 443 6

© Wallace Benn

Published in 2000
by
Christian Focus Publications
Geanies House, Fearn,
Ross-shire, IV20 1TW, Great Britain

Cover Design by Owen Daily

PREFACE

This book is far from being the last word on 'Spirituality'. Indeed spirituality can mean almost anything today and our book shelves are lined with devious and often dangerous substitutes of the real thing. This little book is an attempt to get to the heart of true spirituality (which the Oxford Dictionary defines as 'concerned with the spirit; not physical or worldly') as seen in the teaching and life of the Apostle Paul as he spells it out in his most joyful of letters, Philippians. Spirituality is for Paul about 'life in the world which is orientated towards God' rather than 'life undertaken in withdrawal from the world'.[1]

It is all about Jesus, because the conviction of this book is that it is only as we come to Him who is the Way, the Truth, and the Life that we discover why we were made, what our purpose is in being here, how we can know the God who gives us life, and find peace, forgiveness, hope and a future in Him.

The work of the Holy Spirit, who delights to bring us to Christ to worship and serve Him, is the one who convinces us where true spirituality can be found.

The book does not attempt to be a detailed

commentary on Philippians, but it does seek to faithfully expound the key teaching and themes of Philippians, because true spirituality must be Bible centred, and informed by Holy Scripture.

I am so grateful for the help of Deborah Kelly who originally transcribed the sermons, and edited them, out of which this book came. Also, as ever, many thanks to Malcolm Maclean and the good folk at Christian Focus Publications.

Wallace Benn
Eastbourne
Pentecost 1999

Foreword

On a personal note –

None of us would volunteer for a dose of long-term illness if it were on offer – our view of sickness is usually negative and disabling. But this book was born out of such a time.

One evening three years ago, out of the blue Wallace was struck with a very high fever. We suspected summer 'flu but were to begin the long journey of months and months of illness due to Streptococcal infection which left him with a severe arthritic condition. Weeks of lying in bed left Wallace unable to walk and the road to a full recovery has been painfully slow.

C. S. Lewis has often been quoted as saying that pain is 'God's megaphone to rouse a deaf world'.[2] How true this is. God humbled us, stripped us of all dependence on ourselves and taught us many things about Himself. We hung on to God by the fingernails but He had tight hold of us with His everlasting arms.

In this book Wallace shares with you what God began to teach us and has as its base line our need to have a deep relationship with God. May we together get to know God better.

Lindsay Benn

1

COMING TO KNOW CHRIST

All of us are conscious of how pressured people are in modern society. If someone had told me twenty years ago that this would be the case I would not have believed them. I can remember then how people looked forward to having more space in their lives, and how politicians and others predicted a working week of four days, with three days of leisure time each week. But this scenario has not occurred; in fact, it strikes me that many companies are expecting more and more from their employees. Time seems to be at a premium.

A recent survey discovered that people in London do not know their neighbours at all. Apparently, one reason for the situation is that people do not have time to build relationships with their neighbours. Sadly, in the busy-ness of life, relationships have become less important.

Yet in many people's hearts there is a desire for something more than the run of the mill and the materialism and the daily grind. They realise

11

that there's more to life than what can be seen and touched. This longing may be misdirected, but what it does show is that in each human heart there is a void that has to be filled. And in the search for something to fill that void, people are turning to various kinds of spiritualities.

In fact, spirituality can cover all kinds of efforts to fill that void in the human heart, from the spirituality that is wacky and weird and misleading to the spirituality which appreciates creation and the wonder of the beauty of the world. In fact, some who follow the latter type of spirituality say that through enjoying a walk in the countryside they have been led to admire the Creator of such a beautiful world. That in itself is good, provided they go beyond appreciating God as the Creator to knowing Him as their Redeemer.

I read recently the use one person made of one form of spirituality. She first had to 'space clear', so she took off all her jewellery. Then because mirrors in the bedroom block energy, she covered them up. Then she clapped in the corners of the room to disperse static energy. To me, such behaviour is utter nonsense. But it is an example of the new superstition that is developing in people's thinking. And this kind of spirituality so easily neglects true spirituality.

You may ask, 'What is true spirituality?' The answer to that question begins by understanding what the Bible says about God. One wonderful aspect of God is that He is a Trinity, that in the one God there are three persons – the Father, the Son and the Holy Spirit. This is a great mystery that is beyond our abilities to explain and which we would never have known if the Bible had not told us. But since God is a Trinity of three persons it means that He enjoys relationships. And He wants to have a relationship with those who trust in Him. But this relationship we can have with God is a spiritual one.

When God made each of us He made us spiritual persons. But because we are sinners we do not fully appreciate that we are spiritual creatures, made with the potential of knowing God. Therefore we need the Holy Spirit, the third person in the Trinity, to open our minds to understand that we live in God's world and that God made us for a purpose, which is to know Him by having a relationship with Him.

Paul loved to talk about knowing God through His Son Jesus Christ. This is why we will look at Philippians 3:1-9 first. Please read it carefully and especially note verse 8.

Finally, my brothers, rejoice in the Lord! It is no trouble for me to write the same things to you again, and it is a safeguard for you.
²Watch out for those dogs, those men who

13

do evil, those mutilators of the flesh. [3]For it is we who are the circumcision, we who worship by the Spirit of God, who glory in Christ Jesus, and who put no confidence in the flesh – [4]though I myself have reasons for such confidence.

If anyone else thinks he has reasons to put confidence in the flesh, I have more: [5]circumcised on the eighth day, of the people of Israel, of the tribe of Benjamin, a Hebrew of Hebrews; in regard to the law, a Pharisee; [6]as for zeal, persecuting the church; as for legalistic righteousness, faultless.

[7]But whatever was to my profit I now consider loss for the sake of Christ. [8]What is more, I consider everything a loss compared to the surpassing greatness of knowing Christ Jesus my Lord, for whose sake I have lost all things. I consider them rubbish, that I may gain Christ [9]and be found in Him, not having a righteousness of my own that comes from the law, but that which is through faith in Christ – the righteousness that comes from God and is by faith.

Did you notice that Paul begins this section by referring to joy? 'Finally, my brothers, rejoice in the Lord!' And that he identified Jesus Christ to be the Lord and that it was possible to know Him. Look at verses 8 and 10 where Paul writes 'knowing Christ Jesus my Lord' and 'I want to know Christ'. For Paul, knowing Christ and joy go hand in hand. In other words we can never know the joy that God really intends for us until we know Christ, and we'll miss out on the experience of daily joy unless our knowledge of Christ is growing.

So how does experiencing this true spirituality, which will meet our deepest need and will fill up that void in our inner beings, commence? Or, in other words, where does knowing Jesus begin?

Paul came to a point in his life when, like a good accountant, he had to draw up a profit and loss account. He had to take stock of his life, to evaluate what was really valuable and what was valueless.

We all know it is possible to build up an enormous amount of clutter, not only in our homes, but also in our lives. And we know that we can value some things as very important when, in fact, they are worthless. I know someone who went recently to the Antiques Roadshow with an item which he had thought for about thirty years was very valuable. But he was told that the maximum value of it was not more than £5.

Yet sometimes things that we do not value turn out to be very valuable. When I was a student at university I used to help my uncle who was an auctioneer in house and furniture sales. I enjoyed going out with the removal men and helping them collect furniture. I remember going to a farm which was being sold. We thought we had loaded up all the contents, when the owner asked, 'Would you please take the chest of drawers which is in the cowshed?' It had been in the cowshed for a long time, so it was covered with muck and seemed badly damaged. It turned out to be very valuable and sold for £1,800 (this was the 1960s). It was more valuable than the rest of the contents of the farm put together.

Paul, in taking stock of his life, received a shock because he discovered that the things that he valued actually proved to be totally valueless. In fact the things that he'd valued were only rubbish (verse 8).

Much of the 'rubbish' in Paul's life was connected to his *religious practices*. Note, that he was 'circumcised on the eighth day'. At exactly the right time and in exactly the right way according to the laws of Israel, he was circumcised. This ancient practice was an initiation rite whereby a person showed that they were part of the community of God's people. Circumcision was the Old Testament counterpart to baptism in the New Testament. You know, many people have said to me over the years, 'I've been baptised and confirmed.

I've had everything done to me that the church wants me to have done to me. Therefore I am sure I am a Christian.'

But Paul realised that wearing the badge of believing was no good without the reality of believing. It is good to be baptised – indeed baptism is a visual aid reminding us of God's love and our need to trust and follow Jesus. Yet we must remember that in God's eyes these religious activities do not of *themselves* make us to be right with Him. Without faith they do not impress Him (see Hebrews 4:2 and 11:6).[3] And so Paul learned to put all his religious activities, as a means of impressing God, into the rubbish bin.

But in addition to his religious practices Paul also enjoyed a *privilege of race*. He belonged to 'the people of Israel'. It was a great privilege to be one of the professing people of God, to have the law of God. The Israelites were the only people in the world at that time to have the Bible (the Old Testament). And it is a privilege to hear and to have God's Word. But similar to what he discovered about his religious practices, Paul also discovered that his racial privileges were not enough either to make him right with God. So he had to bin it as just so much rubbish.

Paul also had a strong *spiritual pedigree*, he was 'of the tribe of Benjamin, a Hebrew of Hebrews; in regard to the law, a Pharisee'. Paul belonged to a very important tribe in Israel. It was from his tribe that the first king of Israel had come. And he was also a Pharisee, one of the spiritual elite who imagined they could please God by their own efforts to keep His laws. In fact, as a Pharisee, he thought he was outwardly blameless. But he came to see that, in God's eyes, these things were not impressive. In reality, his efforts to try and please God only showed his frailty and failings and sinfulness, and that he could not live up to God's holiness and perfection. And so he needed to bin his spiritual pedigree as well.

Paul was also very *zealous*. It is very common to hear people say, 'If you're sincere about your religion, that is all that God wants. At the end of the day if you've been zealous and sincere, God will accept you.' But listen to what Paul says: 'as for zeal persecuting the church.' You see, zeal can be misdirected. Zeal and sincerity are not enough in God's eyes. So Paul had to bin *zealousness* as well.

I mentioned earlier that Paul claimed to be outwardly faultless with regard to the claims of God's law. But what about Paul's inward motivation? He saw that God's requirements were not satisfied by mere outward conformity to His laws. In his heart and mind he failed to keep God's law. So he had to cast his internal abilities away as rubbish as well.

I like this comment of William Lane:

'This collapse of self confidence is the essence of faith from a human point of view. It is an expression of confidence in the achievement of Jesus Christ alone.'[4]

We live in a world which is brimming over with self confidence and if we are to know Christ, to know the living God, there has to be a collapse of our arrogant self confidence. We need to understand that we cannot gain God's approval by our religious activities. We cannot find the answer to our deepest needs until we have seen how poor we actually are spiritually. It is then that we will come to the foot of the cross and see what God offers us freely in Jesus.

You see, Paul came to understand that the heart of Christianity is not religiosity, but is a relationship with Jesus. Look at what he says in verse 8: 'the surpassing greatness of knowing Christ Jesus *my* Lord.' Note the little word in italics – the personal pronoun *my*. That's what being truly spiritual is about. It is knowing God through His Son, Jesus. It is to know Him in a personal way.

Paul also discovered that God has a righteousness (verse 9) which He gives freely and is received by the empty hands of faith.

What happens is this. Jesus, God's perfect Son, died for me on the cross and took the penalty of my rottenness and my sinfulness upon Himself so that I might be made right with God. I love this comment of Alec Motyer's: 'We reach the goal of heaven and being acceptable to God, not by the stairs but by the lift.'[5] It is not by the self effort of struggling up the stairs to try and impress God and gain His approval, but it is by the lift of God's grace, in which He takes us freely to heaven, giving us salvation in His Son. Without Christ's death for us we would be lost eternally.

Paul came to the point of seeing that what he could never achieve by his own merit or effort God had offered freely in His Son who had died for him, in his place and as his substitute. The resurrection of Jesus had displayed beyond doubt who Jesus really was – the living, loving, victorious Son of God who is the Saviour of all who turn to Him.

'The cross of Christ stands radically opposed to all religious and ethical presumption which seeks to achieve by works what can only be given through faith.'[6]

So Paul turned away from dependence on anything other than Christ, and all He had done for Him, as a means of getting right with God and of knowing Him. The Bible regularly calls that turning, repentance (literally a change of mind and heart). Paul turned around and put his full confidence and trust in Jesus as his Saviour, Friend, and Lord, and began to follow Him. If we are to know Christ too, like Paul we need to come to that point also. 'Come, follow Me' is the heart of the invitation from Christ. And what joy following Him brings!

The issue in knowing God is not your spiritual pedigree, it is not how long you have been coming to church or whether you had Christian parents. Rather, the issue is, Do you know Jesus Christ? Have you laid aside all your self importance and self pretension and self worth in terms of your ability to achieve God's approval of your life and instead clung to the cross and accepted God's love for you in sending His Son to die for you? That's where knowing Christ begins.

2

KNOWING CHRIST

In chapter one we discussed how a person comes to know Christ. But that experience is only the beginning of a spiritual relationship with Jesus. It is possible to know Him better as time goes by. And it is this possibility that Paul describes in Philippians 3:10-17:

[10]I want to know Christ and the power of His resurrection and the fellowship of sharing in His sufferings, becoming like Him in His death, [11]and so, somehow, to attain to the resurrection from the dead.

[12]Not that I have already obtained all this, or have already been made perfect, but I press on to take hold of that for which Christ Jesus took hold of me. [13]Brothers, I do not consider myself yet to have taken hold of it. But one thing I do: Forgetting what is behind and straining toward what is ahead, [14]I press on

toward the goal to win the prize for which God has called me heavenward in Christ Jesus.

¹⁵All of us who are mature should take such a view of things. And if on some point you think differently, that too God will make clear to you. ¹⁶Only let us live up to what we have already attained.

¹⁷Join with others in following my example, brothers, and take note of those who live according to the pattern we gave you.

Note that in verse 10 Paul says that he still wants to know Christ, even although he began to know Him at his conversion. I think four words will help us understand what Paul has in mind. They are aim, ambition, attainment, and altitude. Let me say something brief about each of them.

Paul describes his *aim* in verses 10 and 11. Sadly, many Christians who have the privilege of knowing Jesus Christ, neglect their relationship with Him. Their aim is not to know Jesus Christ better. They are not making the time in their busy lives to find this oasis that will sustain them and bring them joy in Christian living. Remember joy is connected with knowing Christ, and joy in daily Christian living is connected with knowing Christ better.

It is tragic to see a neglected relationship. I'm sure we have met people who do not put much effort into their marriage relationship. And it leads to a strained relationship. They have not realised that the marriage ceremony is only the beginning. In fact, the ceremony only creates the situation where it is possible to produce a stable lifelong relationship in which the husband and wife get to know one another better and come to love one another more. In marriage there's a joy in discovering things about one another and growing in love and relationship.

The possibility of knowing Christ is similar to an aircraft flight. Sometimes, as the plane takes off, it flies through rain clouds at low level and the visibility is poor. But eventually the plane passes beyond the clouds and the rain into the sunshine. And it is totally different up there! God has given to believers the capacity to get to know Jesus better, to fly, as it were, at 35,000 feet in our Christian lives. Yet some Christians are happy to stay at 5,000 feet with the resulting poorer visibility of Jesus.

Paul's aim was to know Christ better. He was not content with a testimony that only included what had happened when he became a Christian. Or even what the Lord had done for him last year. In fact, a Christian should be able to say what he has learned from the Lord yesterday. How rich our church fellowship would be if each member had an up-to-date testimony of his relationship with Jesus!

But how do we know Christ more intimately? By 'the power of His resurrection and the fellowship of sharing in His sufferings'. We experience His power through the work of the Holy Spirit who enables us to live for Jesus through all the challenges of life, even through suffering and pain and heartache.

This is all part of taking up the cross and following Jesus. *The Christian life is cruciform in character*.[7] It is true that the Christian life is motivated by the love of Christ for us on the cross. But it is also about our taking up the cross daily in following Him. To live for Christ this side of glory was never promised to be easy. We will be derided and misunderstood because we are Christians. We will have to go through difficulties and heartaches. Just as happened to our Saviour, there will be pain and disappointment and difficulty.

Christians are very foolish to think that they will escape from this kind of situation. The health and wealth gospel which promises health and wealth for a Christian is naïve and untrue and unbiblical. Many Christians are thrown off course by suffering and difficulty, but they should not be. We have not been promised to be relieved from difficulties on this side of glory. It is a mercy when God brings healing and help or whatever. But remember there is no guarantee of that as long as we are here in this world. It is in heaven that God will take away the tears from our eyes. It is only in heaven that Kleenex will go out of business!

A doctor said to me recently that we are the first generation in world history to expect health and wealth and ease. But it is no more our right than any previous generation. Christians are not absolved from problems.

I remember being at a meeting of a group of church leaders during which we had a time of discussion regarding the way the Lord had been dealing with us over the previous months. The phrase that kept recurring was 'the blessing of adversity'. We again realised that it is through suffering that God best teaches His people. I remember myself that, during the first six months of my illness, there were days when all that I could do was read three or four psalms a day. But I found that God in His mercy was making these psalms, that I'd always loved, come alive to me in a new way – and the presence of Jesus was so wonderful. On one of the worst days, I was reading a verse that said God rides upon the clouds. As I looked out the window, there were clouds racing across the skies and I reflected, 'How wonderful that the God who made the clouds is the God who loves me and has heaven planned for me. How great it is to know Him.' God in mercy seemed to blaze the relevance of the psalms into my heart, and Jesus was very near. Although I would not wish to have to go through that particular period again in a physical sense, I would not trade those weeks, in which I enjoyed a special sense of the Lord's presence, for anything.

God teaches us through adversity. Consider Psalm 84:5-6: 'Blessed are those whose strength is in You, who have set their hearts on pilgrimage. As they pass through the valley of Baca, they make it a place of springs; the autumn rains also cover it with pools.' The valley of Baca refers to the dry and arid patches in your life, the times that are difficult and hard. God doesn't guarantee that we will be spared adversity. But He does promise His powerful presence.

And Paul adds in verse 11 that he knows that one day in the future God will resurrect him from the dead. Instead of having a frail body he will have a powerful body in which there will be no weaknesses or defects. What a perspective that puts on present suffering!

Paul's great aim was to know Christ better. Therefore he was willing for God, in the school of life, to teach him through the heartaches as well as through the good times. He longed to experience God's power helping him to live for Christ.

The second idea of the four I mentioned above is Paul's *ambition*. In verses 12-14 he uses athletic imagery: 'I press on toward the goal to win the prize for which God has called me heavenward' (verse 14); 'I press on to take hold of that for which Christ Jesus took hold of me' (verse 12).

Paul's ambition was to win the prize at the end of the race. He wanted to get to the end of his life's journey and, at the ticker tape at the end, when he would see his Saviour face to face, to hear Jesus say to him, 'Well done, good and faithful servant.' That was what he coveted more than anything else. That was his greatest ambition.

There is nothing wrong with ambition – the question really is, what is our own main ambition? What motivates more than anything else? Other ambitions have their place, but how foolish to have an ambition dominating our lives that will prove of no value in the end. Someone has rightly said, 'I have never seen a tombstone with the inscription, "I wish I had spent more time in the office!"'

Dear fellow-Christian, what is your over-riding ambition? Is it your boss' approval? Is it a human achievement award? Is it success in life? Is it a big bank balance? If such are your main priorities in life, then you have the wrong ambition. Paul's greatest ambition was to win the prize from Jesus. And that should be our ambition too.

We have noted that in Paul's outlook there was his aim and his ambition. But thirdly, there was his *attainment* (verses 15-16). 'Only let us live up to what we have already attained,' writes Paul to these Philippian Christians. You see, it is possible to slip back as a Christian. It is possible to be a member of a Bible-teaching church and to have a lot of head knowledge but not live by it. And Paul says, 'Don't slip back. Live up to what you've been learning.'

It is important to talk with other Christians about sermons that have moved you, passages from the Bible that have helped you. How can I put what I am learning into practice? And to regularly ask – how am I doing with putting into practice what I have learned this month, this year. Why not review your life spiritually at the beginning of each year or during Lent? Note encouragements and note weaknesses. Have a 'soul friend' with whom you can talk about how you are doing. Don't get despondent – but look to the Lord for help and watch out for slippage!

And, fourthly, there is the *altitude* in which Paul lived (verses 17-21). This idea may not seem to be in the text, but it is. What was wrong with the people whom Paul describes in verses 17-

19? They lived 'as enemies of the cross of Christ', that is, in self confidence. But look at what actually is the heart of their problem. 'Their mind is on earthly things' (verse 19). They had an altitude problem for they were earthbound rather than heaven focused. And unless our focus is on heaven we will never come to terms with the injustices and problems and heartaches of life. If we don't know where it is that God is taking us, if our focus is not on heaven and on all that God is going to do for us there, we will never live securely through the problems and challenges of life.

Recently I flew to Ireland and back on the same day. On the flight to Ireland there was a headwind of 100 mph. It took the plane an hour and ten minutes to get there, but coming back, with the same wind as a tailwind, the flight took forty minutes. I thought, 'Isn't that like us as Christians? The work of the Holy Spirit is constantly to encourage us to know Christ, but sometimes we will insist on flying against His headwind by making other things the priority of our lives. But when we move with the tailwind of the Holy Spirit, we will love Christ, we will walk with Him, we will learn from Him, and we will know the joy of a deepening relationship with Him.

3

TRUSTING THE FATHER
(Philippians 1:3-14)

I remember hearing the well-known Christian leader and author David Watson say, in the last major public meeting that he took part in before his death, that he had come to understand that the most important thing in life was his relationship with God. It was not, therefore, what he *did* for God. He had learned that all he had done in terms of preaching, in terms of service, was less important than his love relationship with the Lord. It was a moving testimony to hear. I also share that understanding and have tried to ensure that every piece of service for the Lord comes out of my relationship with Him.

But during the period that I was ill I discovered that the Lord was re-teaching me that important lesson. For when our health and our ministry is taken away, you realise afresh what is really important. And what is really important in life, when everything else is stripped away? Only one thing, and that is our relationship with the Lord Jesus Christ.

When we think of the importance of that relationship, why is it that sometimes or maybe often, we neglect that relationship, when it is the thing that is most important? Other things, even doing things for the Lord, become the pre-occupying centre of interest in our lives. And yet doing things for the Lord, if it does not come out of a loving relationship with Him, will not be what He intends.

So if our relationship with the Lord is critical and crucial and the most important thing, how do we avoid neglecting the building of that relationship? Or to put it the other way around, how do we grow in that relationship? That is the subject I will try to deal with in this chapter.

Another way to describe this relationship from the Christian's point of view is 'trusting in God' or 'living by faith'. Just as we came into the Christian life through faith (as we trusted in God's provision for our salvation in the death of His Son), so we must remember we are called to go on living by faith day by day.

How can we grow in our faith, in practically trusting God every day? I believe that we can grow in trusting God by living in the light of three great truths, each of which is found in Philippians One. Please read the following scripture passage, and see if you can find these three great truths. They are truths that gave to Paul tremendous confidence and joy in God.

³I thank my God every time I remember you. ⁴In all my prayers for all of you, I always pray with joy ⁵because of your partnership in the gospel from the first day until now, ⁶being confident of this, that He who began a good work in you will carry it on to completion until the day of Christ Jesus.

⁷It is right for me to feel this way about all of you, since I have you in my heart; for whether I am in chains or defending and confirming the gospel, all of you share in God's grace with me. ⁸God can testify how I long for all of you with the affection of Christ Jesus.

⁹And this is my prayer: that your love may abound more and more in knowledge and depth of insight, ¹⁰so that you may be able to discern what is best and may be pure and blameless until the day of Christ, ¹¹filled with the fruit of righteousness that comes through Jesus Christ — to the glory and praise of God.

¹²Now I want you to know, brothers, that what has happened to me has really served to advance the gospel. ¹³As a result, it has become clear throughout the whole palace guard and to everyone else that I am in chains for Christ. ¹⁴Because of my chains, most of the brothers in the Lord have been encouraged to speak the word of God more courageously and fearlessly.

The first great truth is *a confident trust in God's sovereignty over the circumstances of life*. Look at what Paul says to the Philippians in verse 12: 'Now I want you to know, brothers, that what has happened to me has really served to advance the gospel. As a result, it has become clear throughout the whole palace guard and to everyone else that I am in chains for Christ. Because of my chains, most of the brothers in the Lord have been encouraged to speak the word of God more courageously and fearlessly.'

Paul was under house arrest, probably in Rome. Several times he mentions his chains (verses 12, 13, 17). In fact, he was chained to a Roman guard for four hours at a time, when the guard would be replaced. Paul used the opportunity to engage in one-to-one evangelism with these Roman soldiers. Although Paul was chained, God's Word was not chained. In fact, what had happened to Paul had rather served to advance the gospel.

Imagine we are involved in a city-wide evangelistic campaign. It is Day One, the workers are trained, the stadium is booked – and we learn that the evangelist is taken ill. All of a sudden we have to change the plans for the campaign. Paul had wanted to go to Rome to declare Christ there. And now he is in Rome but he is imprisoned. Can you imagine how Christians in Rome would have felt? They would have seen

Paul's imprisonment as a restriction on the work of the gospel. They would be asking, 'Why has God allowed this to happen?'

I remember feeling a bit like this in one of my previous parishes. We had arranged a mission, and a Bible College had agreed to send a team of six students to help us. But we were only one day into the mission when the leader of the student team, the one who was going to do most of the public speaking during the week, had to leave because of ill health. The mission seemed in crisis and we arranged an emergency prayer meeting! And I'm sure that the Christians who knew about Paul's situation had several emergency prayer meetings, asking the Lord to deliver Paul.

But Paul says that he wants them to know that what has happened to him has rather served to advance the gospel. They needed to realise that the circumstances in Paul's life were not outside God's control. Paul could see that God had a reason for allowing him to be imprisoned.

We cannot always see what God's purposes are. With regard to some of the things that God allows to happen to us we will not know the reasons for them until God informs us of them in heaven. But, very often, on looking back on our lives we can see God's hand in what has happened to us.

Paul realised that one reason why God

35

allowed him to be imprisoned was because it gave to Paul opportunities for clear witness about Jesus to the palace guard. And these soldiers had told others about their unusual prisoner, and so throughout the whole palace guard, in the Roman Imperial Court, everyone knew why he was in chains. Perhaps some found Christ (see 4:22)!

You see, at this particular time Christians were actually beginning to suffer for their faith. They were being persecuted because they denied the lordship of Caesar. For them there was only one Lord – Jesus. Here was the great power of the ancient world saying to believers, 'You must bow down to Caesar as Lord.' But here is Paul saying, 'Actually the Lord is breaking into Caesar's household with good news. They cannot contain Him. They cannot restrict those who know Him. What has happened to me has rather served the advancement of the gospel in terms of an opportunity for me to share in an area I might never have got into otherwise.'

'And furthermore,' says Paul, 'there were other Christians in Rome who could preach the gospel but did not feel that they needed to while I was free to do so. But now that I am imprisoned under house-arrest, they have got involved. My imprisonment has also served to advance the gospel since more people are preaching. Because I'm out of the way, more people have come forward and have been encouraged to speak the word of God more courageously and fearlessly. Things are not outside God's control. I can see, I can understand what He is doing in this situation.'

Paul was not thrown by difficult, discouraging circumstances. He believed in a God who is sovereign, who is in control, who is working out His purposes.

There are many verses in the Psalms that indicate the psalmists' confidence in a sovereign God. For example, in Psalm 31:14-15 the writer says: 'But I trust in You, O LORD; I say, "You are my God." My times are in Your hands.' Because Paul, too, shared that confidence he was not thrown by difficult circumstances.

But not only was he not thrown by the difficult circumstances he was going through, neither was he thrown by his disappointment with the behaviour of some believers. Philippians 1:15-18 is a remarkable passage. Paul was very encouraged by the behaviour of those who were preaching the gospel from goodwill, seeking to proclaim Jesus Christ. But, unbelievably, there were other Christians who were actually preaching Christ 'out of selfish ambition, not sincerely, supposing that they can stir up trouble for me while I am in chains' (1:17). Their gospel work was designed by them to cause more problems for Paul. But look at

Paul's positive and magnanimous response in verse 18: 'But what does it matter? The important thing is that in every way, whether from false motives or true, Christ is preached. And because of this I rejoice.' Paul was not thrown by disappointment with the behaviour of some believers.

Not only can we be thrown by difficult, hard circumstances in our health or work or family, but we can be disappointed by the behaviour of other believers. And, of course, other believers are sometimes disappointed with us! But Paul has a confidence in God that is not thrown by the difficulties of life.

But there is another aspect to Paul's perspective on the sovereignty of God. Not only is God working out His purpose for a bigger evangelistic opportunity, but Paul has not lost his confidence of God's purpose for him personally in these difficult circumstances:

'I will continue to rejoice, for I know that through your prayers and the help given by the Spirit of Jesus Christ, what has happened to me will turn out for my deliverance. I eagerly expect and hope that I will in no way be ashamed, but will have sufficient courage so that now as always Christ will be exalted in my body, whether by life or by death' (verses 18-20).

Paul was confident in the ability of God's grace to see him through. He is aware that God has a purpose for him despite the adverse situation he is in. Paul is not even thrown by the possibility of a martyr's death.

Death is the taboo subject in the Western world today. Nobody talks about it. It has been said that 'sex' was the taboo subject of the Victorian era, and in a similar way 'death' is the taboo subject of the late twentieth century. Of course, the reason why no one wants to talk about it is because it frightens them. But Christians have a hope for life beyond death. Look at what Paul says in verses 21-24:

> 'For to me, to live is Christ and to die is gain. If I am going to go on living in the body, this will mean fruitful labour for me. Yet what shall I choose? I do not know! I am torn between the two: I desire to depart and be with Christ, which is better by far; but it is more necessary for you that I remain in the body.'

Our Lord Jesus is the sovereign Lord over death. In fact, death cannot take me away from His love, for it is through death I go to be with Him and to see Him face to face.

Another possible source of deflecting Christians from following Jesus is antagonism from those who oppose the Christian faith. Look at verses 27-30:

> 'Then, whether I come and see you, or only hear about you in my absence, I will know that you stand firm in one spirit, contending as one man for the faith of the gospel, without being frightened in any way by those who oppose you. This is a sign to them that they will be destroyed, but that you will be saved – and that by God. For it has been granted to you on behalf of Christ not only to believe on Him, but also to suffer for Him, since you are going through the same struggle you saw I had, and now hear that I still have.'

You see, here is Paul confident in a God who is in control of his life and his times. His life is in God's hands. His God can be trusted because He is working His purposes out for His glory and the good of His people.

And I too am to recall that God can be trusted because He is working out His purposes for my good. This is not always the way I see it, and perhaps not always the way I want things to be, but it is the way that is best for me.

Paul describes a confident, trustful, joyful delight in a sovereign God who is in control of the circumstances of our lives. And that kind of confident trust in God's sovereignty brings sanity to our Christian living. It is the first key great truth that we need to take hold of, if we are to learn to live by trust in God.

But to only see God's power and sovereignty could leave us overawed. And sometimes in our hurt and sadness we will need to reflect on another great truth which is just as important as appreciating the sovereignty of God. Not only should we have a confident trust in God's sovereignty over the circumstances of our lives, but we also need *a confident trust in God's fatherly care*. And that is the second great truth in this passage.

Look at what Paul says in 1:2: 'Grace and peace to you from God our Father and the Lord Jesus Christ.' What a marvellous greeting! Grace and peace are an encapsulation of all that the gospel gives when a person becomes a Christian. As Paul puts it in Romans 5, we stand in God's grace, we become surrounded by His undeserved love to us. God accepts us into His family and we are able to stand, rather than cower, before Him. We are His children, accepted because of Christ's death for us. We have peace with Him; no longer is there hostility between us. We are brought into a new relationship with God and now travel on the road to glory where, one day, we will enjoy all the fullness of all that Christ has won for us by His death.

In verse 2 Paul combines the Greek greeting (grace) and the Jewish greeting (peace), but in the process he infuses them with Christian significance. This is a simple illustration of what happens to those who become Christians. Much of the mundane and the ordinary in life is transformed by trusting Christ and knowing Him day by day. There's a line in an old hymn which says 'something lives in every hue, Christless eyes have never seen'. When we know that our life is in God's hands, and that we are surrounded by His loving care and His fatherly goodness, it transforms the mundane into the magnificent.

Paul is confident regarding God's fatherly care of the Philippian believers: 'being confident of this, that He who began a good work in you will carry it on to completion until the day of Christ Jesus' (1:6). Paul believed in a Father whose loving care never gives up on the job that He begins. When God puts His hand on a person to save him, He doesn't give up on him until He brings him to glory.

When I was a curate in Cheadle, our house was very cold. Eventually the church decided to put in some loft insulation and double glazing. In November the double glazing man came. I asked him, 'How long will you take to do it?' Looking at me with a kind of disdain he replied, 'We will be finished by Friday.' This was on

Monday in the first week in November. They actually finished the work during the first week in April! And even when they said they were finished there were still holes in the spaces around some of the windows.

But God is not like that. When He sets His hand to do something, He brings it to completion. We can trust our Father who planned our redemption before the universe was made. I can trust Him to work for His glory and for my good as He sees it. I can really trust His fatherly care in the circumstances of life.

I regularly use one of C H Spurgeon's books of daily readings. During my period of illness, especially in the November of that year, we were feeling particularly low, with no further information medically regarding my problem. Let me share with you the reading of November 11th which is based on Psalm 47:4: 'He shall choose our inheritance for us.' This is what Spurgeon wrote:

'Unerring wisdom ordained your lot and selected for you the safest and best condition. A ship of large tonnage is to be brought up the river. Now in one part of the stream there is a sandbank. Should someone ask, "Why does the captain steer through the deep part of the channel and deviate so much from a straight line?", his answer would be,

"Because I should not get my vessel into harbour at all if I did not keep to the deep channel." So it may be you would run aground and suffer shipwreck, Christian, if your divine captain did not steer you into the depths of affliction, where waves of trouble follow each other in quick succession. Remember this – had any other condition been better for you than the one in which you are, divine love would have put you there. You are placed by God in the most suitable circumstances.'

The picture of the deep channel through which the captain had to steer the boat in order to get into the safe harbour is a brilliant analogy of how God brings us through hard times and difficult circumstances and deep affliction. It is through such that God works His purposes out in the way that is best for His glory and for our good. Spurgeon concludes with a verse from a hymn:

> Trials must and will befall,
> but with humble faith to see
> Love inscribed upon them all.
> This is happiness to me.[8]

I have found the following comment of J. I. Packer to be helpful. Commenting on Judges

13 he says: 'Sometimes what God seems to promise us seems to be denied by the circumstances of our lives. The hopes God has given were truly fulfilled in the story in Judges 13, though not in the way that was first expected. Panic reactions at times of stress and trauma will lead us infallibly to wrong conclusions as Christians.'[9]

So when we're in the midst of adversity and trouble and distress and heartache, we can panic. But Paul did not panic because he looked up to a God who was in sovereign control, but also a God whose fatherly care he knew.

So we have seen that our relationship with God will grow as we trust in His sovereignty and in His fatherly care. But there is also a third truth about our relationship with God that Paul refers to in this passage, and it is *a confident trust in God's loving presence and help.*

Look again at Paul's expectation in verses 19 and 20. He believes that in this particular situation, God will deliver him, that He will bring him out of prison. And so it happened. Some time later Paul was re-arrested and executed. But he was freed from the imprisonment he was undergoing when he wrote this letter to the Philippians. But until that happened Paul knew it was possible he might not be released. But whether he would be released or not he would continue to trust his heavenly Father. For he knew that God would not fail him.

Paul is confident that God's resources will be there for him. And he mentions two important aspects of how God will enable him to continue serving in whatever circumstances he finds himself.

The first aspect is the prayers of the Philippians for him. He knew that his God is the heavenly Father who both answered Paul's prayers and also led other believers to pray for him and answer their prayers too.

The second aspect is described in the lovely phrase: 'and the help given by the Spirit of Jesus Christ', which I prefer to translate literally as 'the supply of the Spirit of Jesus Christ'. What does Paul mean? He means that the supply of the Holy Spirit, the personal presence of God with me, will never run out. He will be totally sufficient in every situation. What He gives will be totally adequate for Paul. He will never dry up or run out or fail to be there when Paul needs Him. God graciously gives us His wonderful, helpful, joyful Spirit and we can rely on His help. And that has been the testimony down the years of many, many Christians.

There is another great verse from the Psalms that I want to refer to because I think it sums up the joyful confidence of Philippians Chapter One. The verse is Psalm 138:8: 'The LORD will fulfil His purpose for me.' Or as the New Living Translation puts it: 'The Lord will work out His plans for my life, for Your faithful love, O Lord, endures forever.' Because of God's gracious love to me, I can trust Him that He will work out His plans for me.

So let us learn to live by trust in God. This is what living by faith means. We need to have confidence in a sovereign, loving, heavenly Father who will stand by us and be with us by His Spirit. We need to feed our hearts and minds on what the Bible says about our great God. We need to treasure up verses like Psalm 138:8, by actually memorising them and preaching them to ourselves when we're tempted to doubt God's love and when we're made despondent by the circumstances of life. As we do we will know the joy and the strength and the confidence that will transform the difficult or the mundane into wonderful experiences on the pathway to heaven.

4

CHRISTLIKE SERVICE
(Philippians 2:5-18)

In this chapter we are going to consider Philippians
Two. But the key verse is verse 5: 'Your attitude
should be the same as that of Christ Jesus.'

One of the saddest things to see is a wasted
life. But we need to ask ourselves a very
important question: 'What is the secret of a
useful life that is fulfilled and worthwhile?'

I remember talking to someone who had
become a Christian in his sixties. With tears in
his eyes and with great sadness, he said to me,
'I've wasted so many years. I've wasted so much
of my life by not knowing Jesus Christ. Would
that I had known Him earlier.' But he is actually
funnelling into his last years so much for the
Lord.

But what is the secret of a useful life? In
Philippians 2 Paul gives two notable examples.
The first example is Timothy (verses 19-20).
Paul says, 'I have no one else like him.' Amongst
the early Christians, Timothy was exceptional.
The second example is Epaphroditus (verse 25),
whom Paul describes as 'my brother, fellow

worker and fellow soldier, who is also your messenger'. What a delightful description of another Christian: We are to 'honour men like him because he almost died for the work of Christ'.

What made Timothy and Epaphroditus exceptional? They were Christians, yet even amongst the Christians they were noteworthy and exceptional. Why was that? If we are to see the point of this chapter, we need to follow the flow of Paul's argument.

Four marks of being a Christian
In verse 1 Paul mentions four marks of a Christian, each indicated by the little word *if*: '*If* you have any encouragement from being united with Christ, *if* any comfort from His love, *if* any fellowship with the Spirit, *if* any tenderness and compassion...' The word *if* does not mean that Paul doubted their genuine Christianity, rather it means 'since' or 'as sure as'.[10]

Encouragement from being united with Christ. Being united with Jesus Christ means that all the promises of God in Christ become ours. Because we are united with the One who is the conqueror of death, we have the life that He came to bring us. To be loved by Him and owned by Him and identified with Him, isn't that an encouragement?

Comfort from His love. What a comfort the

love of Christ is. His love for us led Him to die for us on the cross. The fact that He loves us indicates we have value in the eyes of God. What a comfort it is to know, in the ups and downs and the challenges and the heartaches of life, that He loves us with an everlasting love. His love never fails.

Fellowship with the Spirit. This phrase refers to the joy of knowing the presence of God with us day by day, of *koinonia* with God Himself. It means being able to stand at a bus-stop or at a sink or in a classroom or in a pulpit, or wherever and knowing the presence and the peace of God, with the strength of the Holy Spirit enabling us to do what God calls us to do.

Tenderness and compassion. In Ephesians 4:17-19 Paul describes what it means to be outside Christ, to be an unbeliever. One of the things he says about unbelievers is that they are futile in their thinking. They can't think straight about the world, about why they are here, because they do not know God. The second thing Paul says there about unbelievers is that there is a hardness in their hearts, a hardness of heart because of self absorption. But when a person becomes a Christian God begins to tenderise him and to soften his heart. What a good thing that is, when God begins to tenderise a person, and make him compassionate and concerned for others.

Paul says that these four marks will be found in all who are Christians. Therefore, he asks the Philippian believers to 'make my joy complete by being like-minded, having the same love, being one in spirit and purpose' (verse 2). Are you encouraged by what God has done for you and is doing for you? Then, have a unity of mind and heart with other Christians that pulls together in the same direction – in the direction in which God wants all His people to go.

Today we live in a world where often we hear about attitude problems. What Paul is talking about here is having the right attitude, the right mindset, to put it another way. Isn't it true that there are basically two kinds of people? On the one hand there are those who believe that the world owes them something, who are primarily concerned about their rights and their privileges and their concerns and their agendas. And, on the other hand, there are those who want to make a difference by their lives in the world and in the generation in which they live, who see their primary concern not to be what they can get, but rather what they can give and contribute.

So Paul says that he wants them to have the kind of 'one spirit and purpose' that does 'nothing out of selfish ambition or vain conceit' (verse 3). Of course, there is nothing wrong with ambition, if our ambition is to serve God and

51

go His way. The ambition Paul condemns is selfish ambition, that horrible, self-centred, self-absorbed ambition, with its vain conceit, that is, its viewing itself more highly than it ought, which comes from a heart full of pride and which will cause trouble. But a Christian who is indebted to the love and mercy of God ought to have a different mindset. In fact, Christians are to have the same attitude as that of Jesus Christ, who is our model and our example.

A different attitude – that of Jesus Christ
Now what exactly is the attitude of Christ? What is the mindset of Jesus Christ? That's what Paul turns to in verses 5-11, which is, according to many scholars, a magnificent early Christian hymn. Alec Motyer writes concerning it:

> 'The present passage uniquely unfolds the cross as seen through the eyes of the Crucified, and allows us to enter into the mind of Christ. We tread, therefore, on very holy ground indeed.'[11]

The only parallel passage to verses 5 to 11, that I can think of in the New Testament, is John 13. There John tells us the very mindset of the Lord Jesus, as He approached the cross. In that incident Jesus showed His humility by taking a towel and washing His disciples' feet. That task

52

was usually done by a slave. What Jesus did there in the Upper Room is a picture of what He did in becoming a man. Paul describes the descent of Christ in Philippians 2:5-8, before describing His exaltation in verses 9-11. I think it is worth pointing out that in verses 5-8 the emphasis is on what Jesus did, whereas in verses 9-11 the emphasis changes to what the Father did for Jesus. Let me comment briefly on each phrase in this magnificent poem.

Who, being in very nature God. This means that Jesus is, in fact, really God. He is, as Hebrews 1:3 puts it, 'the exact representation of His being'. Literally here the word is the imprint of a stamp. Jesus is to the Father as the imprint of a stamp is to the stamp itself!

did not consider equality with God something to be grasped. The New Living Translation gets the gist of this clause absolutely right: 'though He was God, He did not demand and cling to His rights as God.' Jesus could have stayed in heaven, enjoying His privileges as the second person of the Trinity without blame. And yet He laid aside His rights and His reputation to come to earth and go to the cross for us.

One of the most delightful comments that I came across, and which has been a real blessing to me is this: 'Jesus viewed equality with God not about getting, but on the contrary about giving.'[12]

53

but made Himself nothing. Literally this phrase means 'He emptied Himself'. Again to quote Alec Motyer: 'The question is not "Of what did He empty Himself?", He didn't empty Himself of Godhood, but "Into what did He empty Himself?" '[13]

He emptied Himself by *taking the very nature of a servant.* The word 'nature' is the same word as in the first line of verse 6. Jesus became a real servant, having the essential quality of what it means to be a servant. In fact the word 'servant' is too gently translated by the NIV. The word Paul uses is *doulos*, the word meaning 'slave'.

In addition Jesus' emptying Himself included His becoming a real man in time and space: *being made in human likeness. And being found in appearance as a man...* The Incarnation means that He became real flesh and blood, fully human (one of us!), yet without sin. He got tired and hungry just as we do!

And as a man *He humbled Himself and became obedient to death, even death on a cross.* Obedience to God's will was Jesus' prime purpose, even although it involved crucifixion. Cicero described crucifixion as the most cruel and abominable form of punishment. Every Jew knew, 'Cursed is everyone who is hung on a tree' (Deut. 21:23; Gal. 3:13). That the Son of God should humble Himself and become obedient to such a death is staggering. You and I don't have a choice whether we die or not. But Jesus had a choice and He became obedient unto death. 'Only a Divine being can accept death as obedience – for ordinary people it is a necessity' (Lohmeyer).

But because of who He was and because of His loving obedience to His Father's will, *therefore God exalted Him to the highest place and gave Him the name that is above every name, that at the name of Jesus every knee should bow, in heaven and on earth and under the earth, and every tongue confess that Jesus Christ is Lord, to the glory of God the Father.* The name given to Jesus is 'Lord', it is 'the name that is above every name', and is the equivalent of the Old Testament divine name 'Yahweh'. It was used in the Septuagint, the Greek Translation of the Old Testament, as the word to translate Yahweh or Jehovah, translated in most versions as LORD. Jesus is God come in the flesh. And when we acknowledge that Jesus is God, it brings glory to the Father. (See also Isaiah 45:23, where a verse referring to God there is quoted here referring to Jesus.)

In the light of the amazing love of Jesus, Paul says in verses 12-13: 'Therefore, my dear friends, as you have always obeyed – not only in my presence, but now much more in my absence – continue to work out your salvation with fear and trembling, for it is God who works in you to will and to act according to His good purpose.' And working out our salvation involves our mindset and our attitude. What does that mean? It means acting according to God's good purpose. It means co-operating with God's intention for us.

Such an attitude includes *doing everything without complaining or arguing* (verse 14). One of the things that struck me when I went to America a few years ago was how service in our country has deteriorated. Over there, in shops and restaurants, people were polite and helpful. But we live in a society where complaining and arguing has become very common. But Christians are not to be like that. Instead they are to be so different that they stand out from the crowd. They don't serve God with complaining and arguing in their hearts. Rather they stand out as lights for Him; by a different quality of life and attitude, they are shining for Him (verse 15).

Part of their witness involves holding out the word of life. Christians should not be embarrassed at having to speak to others about Christ. They know that there is no life apart from Jesus Christ, be it real life in this world or eternal life in the next world. So as they have opportunity they tell people the good news of the gospel which can bring real life (verse 16).

And notice they are to offer it with joy rather than force it down others throats!

Timothy and Epaphroditus

Paul also uses his two colleagues, Timothy and Epaphroditus, as examples of what he has been urging on believers. I mentioned above how Paul said of Timothy: 'I have no one else like him.' Why was Timothy so unique? Because, as Paul goes on to say, he took 'a genuine interest in your welfare. For everyone looks out for his own interests, not those of Jesus Christ' (verses 20, 21). Too many Christians in Paul's day were self absorbed and self concerned. But Timothy was not like that. He had a genuine interest for the well-being of other Christians. This behaviour developed out of a concern not to make his own interests his primary occupation, but actually to focus on the interests of Jesus Christ and the good of His kingdom.

Epaphroditus was not an easy name with which to live in the Christian community. Aphrodite was, amongst other things, the goddess of gamblers. Imagine being a keen Christian and having your name associated with the goddess of gamblers! Not wonderful, is it? But for Paul, Epaphroditus was 'my brother, fellow worker and fellow soldier, who is also your messenger' (verse 25), who 'almost died for the work of Christ (verse 30). There's a play on words in verses 29 and 30. Here is a man named after the goddess of gamblers, yet who did not gamble in a wrong way, but rather he risked his life to serve the Lord. He bet on a sure thing!

Why are these two Christians mentioned? They are examples of Paul's exhortation, 'Your attitude should be the same as that of Christ Jesus.' Timothy and Epaphroditus had been deeply touched and affected by *the servant heart of Jesus*. Their concern, flowing out of loving gratitude to Jesus Christ for all that He had done for them, was to be like Him. They had been so moved by the One who laid aside all the rights of heaven and instead became a slave with no rights, with a concern to only do the Father's will. They were now the kind of people who did not stand on their rights. They had let go all their rights and all their privileges, and their primary concern now was their Master's wish.

I think Paul's favourite description of himself was 'a slave of Christ Jesus' (1:1). No doubt Timothy and Epaphroditus had seen this mindset in Paul. They saw that Paul found joy and liberty and delight and fulfilment in serving the Lord as His slave.

We live in a society where people are dominated by materialism, where they are possessed by self. But Christians are to have a different attitude and mindset. We need to ask ourselves: do we reflect the attitudes of our day? Perhaps we are almost the same as unbelievers. Or are we as radically different as God calls us to be? Are we mirroring something of the mindset of our Master?

What are our priorities? We can fill our lives with busyness. I'm very aware how busy life has become for some folk and sometimes Christians can do very little about the demands of their employer. But sometimes they stay on at work longer than is necessary in order to impress. When the church says they should make learning about Jesus Christ a priority, or that they also need to be a good father or mother and spend time with their children, they say they are too busy. Such people need to unblock the rubbish in their lives and get their priorities straight.

Some Christian parents fill up their lives with all kinds of organisations for their children. They give them everything but when it comes to church their outlook is so different. Many parents over the years have said to me, 'Our son does not want to come to church any more. We feel it is a sensitive issue for he is eleven years old.' What if their son at the same age said, 'I don't want to brush my teeth anymore.' They would not let him do what he wants in that case. But when it comes to church, somehow it is different.

We need to get our priorities right.

The way of Christ is to serve God out of gratitude. Our obedience to God's will must be our first concern. When we serve Christ and serve others, we will discover that there is freedom, joy and fulfilment in living that way. There is no danger of a wasted life if we dedicate ourselves to the Lord and to His service. You see, if we seek pleasure, if we seek joy, we will miss our goal. But if we seek God and serve Him we will find true pleasure and real joy.

It is a privilege to be called a servant of the One who was our servant unto death. One of the things that struck me during the time I was unable to work because of my ill health, was to see again the immense privilege of being able to serve the living God. And when God changes our attitude and our mindset and makes it like Christ, then like Timothy and like Epaphroditus we will be useful in the hands of God.

'This is our God, the Servant King
He calls us now to follow Him,
To bring our lives as a daily offering
Of worship to the Servant King.'[14]

5

ENJOYING GOD

The experience of joy is the Christian's birthright. It is something that is the peculiar, distinct, and particular privilege of being a Christian. But what exactly is Christian joy? Joy is not to be confused with happiness, because if we are in pain or in difficulty we will not necessarily feel happy, but joy can be there whatever the circumstances we may face. Joy is something much deeper than the coming and going of happiness.

But on the other hand I think that some people have confused deep joy with the kind of experience that never seems to affect the muscles of their faces and enables them to smile! But joy will show in our faces.

Since joy is the Christian's birthright, in this chapter we will think about how we can experience joy as God intends us to.

The book of Philippians is the biblical book *par excellence* about Christian joy. No less than sixteen times in its four chapters does Paul refer to joy. And the section we are going to consider in this chapter is punctuated with references to joy.

There is 3:1: 'Finally my brothers, rejoice in the Lord!'; 4:4 'Rejoice in the Lord always'; and 4:10: 'I rejoice greatly in the Lord.' Notice two things about the phrase 'Rejoice in the Lord'.

Firstly, notice that in two of the three occasions it is in the form of a command. You may ask, 'How can I be commanded to be joyful?' But you see, there is never a circumstance in which a Christian finds himself that there is not adequate reasons to be joyful. And we shall consider this aspect further below.

Then secondly, joy is always connected with the Lord Jesus. In fact, our joy will be as correspondingly deep as we are close to Him. The further we are away from the Lord Jesus, the more will our joy diminish. Christian joy is always *in the Lord*, and we deepen our joy as we draw nearer to Him. This is how Alec Motyer puts it: '[Christ] mediates to us all the benefits and blessings of God. More than that, He is Himself the sum of all the blessings. For Paul, the person who possesses Christ possesses all.'[15] Joy is always connected to focusing on Christ, worshipping Him and serving Him. Joy is cross-centred and resurrection-centred. If we are far away or just beginning to drift away from Jesus, we will have corresponding less joy. It is our closeness to Jesus that brings us joy.

Let us look together at the material found around these three statements concerning joy in the Lord (3:1; 4:4; 4:10) under three headings.

1. The foundations of Christian joy

The foundations of joy are the great truths of the gospel of our Lord and Saviour Jesus Christ. We did consider some of this material in a previous chapter, but let me just remind you of some of the things we noticed.

1. Righteousness through faith in Christ: 'I consider them [that is everything I valued before] rubbish, that I may gain Christ and be found in Him [in union with Him], not having a righteousness of my own that comes from the law, but that which is through faith in Christ – the righteousness that comes from God and is by faith' (3:8, 9).

The first ground of Christian joy is discovering good news after learning of very bad news. The bad news is that we can never earn God's approval, that we can never live up to His standard by our efforts or our spiritual pedigree or by religious observances. Paul, before he became a Christian, was a deeply religious person. But he discovered that in God's eyes he did not meet God's standard. When Paul realised that, he was devastated, but then he discovered something absolutely tremendous. He realised that God gives the supreme delight and joyful privilege of being right with Him freely as a gift. All Paul had to do was receive the gift with the empty hands of faith. What a source of joy!

Personally, if I did not believe in the gospel of Jesus Christ, the good news of a righteousness from God freely given to sinners, I would not want to be religious. Trying to work up an appropriate amount of obedience to God's requirements would not only be impossible, it would be incredibly boring. What a chore mere religiosity is.

Christianity is not about pulling ourselves up by our own bootlaces and trying to earn God's approval. Rather, it is discovering that we cannot do so, but also discovering that God in His love has come to us in His Son and offers us freely an eternal relationship with Him as His children. I am accepted by God because of Christ, and I go on being accepted because of Him. 'He is all my righteousness, I stand complete in Him, and worship Him.'[16] What a source of joy!

2. *God has put His hand upon my life and has a purpose for me.* In verse 12 Paul says: 'I press on to take hold of that for which Christ Jesus took hold of me.' Jesus has put His hand upon Paul's life, not only as his Saviour from sin, but also as his master and guide through life.

Therefore Paul's life had purpose, it had direction, it had motivation – to live for Jesus.

I recently read a magazine article written by an agnostic. He said, 'I'm not sure whether I'm an agnostic or an atheist. But I want to say this, that modern men and women have an emptiness in life which might only be filled by the message of Christmas.' What an interesting comment! He went on to say, 'I don't believe the message of Christmas. But maybe the emptiness that I feel in my life, and I observe everybody else feels, of purposelessness and lack of direction, can only be filled by the message of Christmas.' As I was reading the article, I kept saying to him, 'Believe it! You see the problem, now go for the solution.'

But Paul knew that his life had purpose and direction and motivation because God had taken hold of it. In 1:6, Paul expressed his confidence that God, who had begun a work in the lives of the Philippian believers, would carry it to completion. And Paul rejoiced that they were responding to God in His work in their lives. They were not resisting Him, rather they were seeking to live for the Lord (1:5).

So there is the second great foundation truth: God has put His hand upon our lives. He has a purpose for each of His people.

In 3:10, Paul spells out what God's purpose for every believer is: 'I want to know Christ ...

becoming like Him.' That's why God has put His hand upon our lives. He intends to deliver us from selfishness and self-centredness, from the folly of our own ways. Instead, He aims to make us more like the Lord Jesus. That is why He has put His hand upon our lives.

3. A destiny – heaven. The third great foundation of gospel joy is described by Paul in verse 14: 'I press on toward the goal to win the prize for which God has called me heavenward in Christ Jesus.'

One of the great privileges given to the inhabitants of Philippi was the right of Roman citizenship. To them was given the same privileges that was given to the inhabitants of Rome. Philippi was in effect a colony of Rome. Paul uses this privilege to illustrate the great dignity that God has given to Christians. In 3:20, he writes: 'But our citizenship is in heaven. And we eagerly await a Saviour from there, the Lord Jesus Christ, who, by the power that enables Him to bring everything under His control, will transform our lowly bodies so that they will be like His glorious body.'

Says Paul, 'God called me heavenward. He has redeemed me, He has saved me from lostness, He has put His hand upon my life and given it direction and purpose. My destiny is heaven, it is my real home. Heaven is where I belong to, it is my homeland. It is where Jesus in His mercy is going to bring me. One day He will transform my lowly body so that it will be like His glorious body.' Says Paul, 'I've got a future!'

No Christian is without a future. No Christian is without a sure hope as he looks into the unknown future. Every Christian has a destiny, has an inheritance waiting for him in heaven. Every Christian can look forward to that great transformation when his frail, sick, sinful body will be transformed. That is terrific!

I recently read, over a period of a few months, Joni Eareckson Tada's book on heaven.[17] It is an absolutely delightful book where Joni looks forward with profound insight into what God is going to do for those who love Him. Joni has been paralysed for over thirty years. Yet her joy at the prospect of what God is going to do for her, and for all His people, fills every page.

So these are three great foundation truths for Christian joy. But let me remind you that each of them is 'in' Christ, and through Christ and because of Christ.

How can I sum up all that I have been saying? The Christian faith is about a relationship with God's Son, a relationship with God through the Lord Jesus Christ where I get to know the living God through His Son. I will get to know Him better through life's ups and downs as I learn to trust Him and realise that He's put His hand upon my life for a purpose. And one day I'll see Him face to face and get to know Him even better.

You see, it is all about *knowing Christ*, it is all about being centred on Him. Joy for a Christian is focusing on Christ and walking with Christ and enjoying all that He has won for us, all that He is doing for us, and all that He will do for us.

2. Hindrances to our Experience of Joy

So, these are the foundations for Christian joy. But in Philippians 4, from verse 2 onwards, Paul mentions four hindrances to Christian joy.

The first is *bad relationships between believers*: 'I plead with Euodia and I plead with Syntyche to agree with each other in the Lord.' Here are two women in the church at Philippi who were a pain to themselves and to one another. Someone has written that they should have been called 'You are odious' and 'You are soon touchy'! These two women were not getting on. So Paul asked a particular individual to help the ladies. The term translated 'loyal yokefellow' may be a proper name, 'Syzygus'.

What is sad about these two women is that when Paul had evangelised Philippi, both Euodia and Syntyche had worked together to serve the Lord and spread the gospel. Paul writes, 'Help these women who have contended at my side in the cause of the gospel.' Now they are taken up with their own disagreement and their own agendas. What a waste!

Many a good work for God has been hindered by bad relationships. I know of a missionary agency that, when I was a boy, had sixty-plus full-time Christian workers. Now it has one full-time and one part-time worker – not because it abandoned doctrine, not because there is no longer a need for the work, but because of a few dominant and hard-to-get-on with personalities who caused problems.

Sometimes the work of God is hindered by those who have not taken the advice of Philippians 2:3: 'Do nothing out of selfish ambition or vain conceit.' Christians can be very taken up with their own concerns and their own desires and wanting to see this or that done, rather than serving God's purpose and looking for His will in the matter.

So bad relationships are a real hindrance to the experience of Christian joy. Maybe you know that there is a cloud between you and another Christian. Perhaps you need to go to that Christian and say, 'I'm sorry.' Even if you don't understand the reason for the cloud, go to the other Christian anyway, and get rid of the problem so that there may be no hindrance in the work of the Lord.

Paul gives another reason why the two women should be enjoying a harmonious relationship. Both their names are 'in the book of life'. Both of them were going to heaven where they were going to spend eternity together. Therefore, they may as well get on here!

The second hindrance to the experience of joy is *worry*. Instead of worrying Paul says: 'Let your gentleness [literally, your forbearing spirit] be evident to all.' How can Paul tell us not to worry, especially if we are, by disposition, the worrying kind of person? Paul gives his grounds at the end of verse 5: 'The Lord is near.' I used to think Paul meant that the Lord's return was near, and to be fair some commentators take this to be Paul's meaning. But I don't think that's what Paul meant. Rather he is saying that the Lord is near, close by us. He never leaves us or forsakes us.

One of the reasons we worry so often in life is because we conclude we will be in a situation that we will not be able to cope with. But Paul reminds believers that the divine resources available to each Christian will not fail. Therefore 'do not be anxious about anything.' Since God's resources are available to us by His ever-present Spirit, why should we worry unduly? John Gwyn-Thomas wrote a great book on Philippians 4 called *Rejoice Always*.[18] In his

70

book he says this: 'The devil does not want us to bring our problems, great or small, to God, because he does not want us to see them in their proper perspective.'

Do you remember when you were growing up and measuring your height to see how you were growing? Sometimes we measure our problems simply by the size of the problem, or by other people's problems. But we should measure the problems by the presence of God with us. And if we measure our problems by God, he's always bigger than our problems.

Listen again to John Gwyn-Thomas: 'The answer to care is prayer'; and again: 'Every anxiety is a personal invitation from God to come before Him in prayer, to call us back into His presence, to talk to Him about it.'[19] So every anxiety, every worry, potentially drives us to our knees and draws us into a deeper, richer fellowship with God as we talk to Him about our worries and as we realise he's with us.

There is both a command and a promise here. Along with the obedience to this command comes the promise of verse 7, that the peace of God will be experienced in our hearts and our lives. Notice how these verses are translated in the New Living Translation:

'Don't worry about anything, instead pray about everything. Tell God what you need

71

and thank Him for all that He's done. If you do this, you will experience God's peace which is far more wonderful than the human mind can understand. His peace will guard your hearts and minds as you live in Christ Jesus.'

I came across recently this terrific quote from William Perkins, one of the Puritans. He said this: 'When thou first openest thy eyes in a morning, pray to God and give Him thanks heartily. God shall then have His honour and thy heart shall be the better for it the whole day following.'[20] Let the first thing in your day be praise of God! If the first thing you do is look in the mirror you may get depressed, look first to God!

Paul here commends not only petition to help anxiety, but also praise. Giving thanks is a key to experiencing joy.

The third hindrance to the experience of joy is connected to the battle going on within every Christian concerning *the battle for the mind*: '...if anything is excellent or praiseworthy – think about such things.' Paul stresses that there is a battle going on for our minds. Therefore we need to be careful as to what we fill our minds with.

Whatever is good in the world, whatever God has made for our pleasure, enjoy and delight in it. Christians should enjoy the beauty of creation, the wonder of art and music. Whatever is noble and worthy and excellent, Christians should think about these things. But they should especially think about God's goodness in the Lord Jesus Christ. Fill your hearts and minds with these things. Be a positive believer, that is, fill your mind with whatever is excellent and praiseworthy.

The fourth hindrance to experiencing joy is the failure to *put into practice*: 'Whatever you have learned or received or heard from me, or seen in me – put it into practice.' A few years ago I had golf lessons from a professional. I didn't need one lesson – I needed about 200! He said to me, 'There's one thing very seriously wrong with your game that is affecting everything else. But behind your problem is the fact that you do not practice enough. You will never get any good at golf unless you swing a club every day.' I said to him that I did not have time to do so. He replied: 'I don't mean that you should have a round every day. Just swing a club every day. Unless you do that you will never get any good at golf.'

The problem with a lot of Christians is that we do not put into practice what we are learning. We have so many privileges, so much information from the Bible. But we grow in joy as we put into practice what we are learning:

'Whatever you have learned or received or heard from me, or seen in me – put it into practice. And the God of peace will be with you' (verse 9).

3. Joy increasing
Paul affirms his outlook in verse 10: 'I rejoice greatly in the Lord.' There are two things here that we need to take note of.

Firstly, Paul received encouragement by the support of other Christians. Paul was so encouraged by fellowship with the Philippian Christians. Look what he says: 'I rejoice greatly in the Lord that at last you have renewed your concern for me' (verse 10); 'Yet it was good of you to share in my troubles' (verse 14); 'not one church shared with me in the matter of giving and receiving, except you only' (verse 15).

Here was a group of Christians who were such an encouragement to Paul. They were concerned for him and were bearing his burdens and sharing his troubles (verse 14). They were the kind of Christians who knew how much they had received from the kindness and generosity of God, whose lives had been affected by God's kindness, and they wanted to show that same kindness to other believers (verse 15). Their behaviour was such an encouragement to Paul, at the edge of missionary endeavour. How encouraged he was in knowing he was supported by these lovely Christians.

We live in a world that has grown harder and more indifferent to human need and suffering. Christians need to be the kind of people who are different, who are aware of how much God has shown them in His kindness, especially in His generosity in giving His Son to die for us. The kindness and generosity that reached its height in the cross of Jesus Christ must be reflected in our lives. We should be going out of our way to be kind to others, going out of our way to show concern for one another as part of the family of believers.

Secondly, Paul's joy increased through *the encouragement of the evidence of God at work in them*. Look what he says in verse 18: 'I have received full payment and even more; I am amply supplied, now that I have received from Epaphroditus the gifts you sent. They are a fragrant offering, an acceptable sacrifice, pleasing to God.' What an encouragement it is to see God at work in another person, to see motivations change and priorities turning upside down. In other words, to see God change lives. To see them delight now in using their resources in the service of God, and for the good of His people.

That is why a Christian who tries to live on his own, and who hangs loose to Christian fellowship, will never grow in joy. If you are not feeling so good spiritually or in any other way, make sure you are at church. When you are not able to pray on your own, that is the very time to be carried along by the prayers of others, that is the very time to make sure that you do not miss out on the support, encouragement, and joy of Christian fellowship. Playing our part in the fellowship of the Church family is essential for growth. It is the place where we learn and are encouraged.

4. Joy in all circumstances

And there is something else here. Look at what Paul writes in verse 11: 'I am not saying this because I am in need, for I have learned to be content whatever the circumstances,' whether he is in a situation of plenty or of want, of feeling well fed or hungry. What a nonsense it is when some people tell us that every Christian has the right to good health and wealth. It's not true. Paul as an apostle, the greatest Christian missionary, knew what it was to be hungry and to suffer loss for Christ.

What was it that enabled him to rise above the circumstances of his life, to keep his equilibrium through the ups and downs of life? I think Alec Motyer grasps Paul's point when he writes: 'He accepted all his circumstances as from God (verses 10, 12, 15) and glorified

God in them all (verse 20).' 'Paul had learned to be content because he had learned to trust.'[21] He had learned to look to God for deliverance from a problem. But even if God was not going to deliver him, he would still trust Him that His grace would be sufficient through it.

Notice that Paul had 'learned' contentment. Do not imagine that this happened overnight. Listen again to John Gwyn-Thomas: 'He had not come to this position easily or quickly. This spiritual learning is a process.'[22] For it is God who is dealing with us in His school of learning. Paul did not learn, overnight, contentment in difficult circumstances. Nor will you and I, in a discontented age, when we seem to have more than ever; and yet whatever we possess, by way of material things actually never make us content.

So we need to learn contentment too. How do we do so? We learn it by trusting in the Lord's providential care, that He is committed to us, that the God who has redeemed us and is bringing us to heaven will not let us down. God can be trusted through the ups and downs of life. That's the gist of what Paul says in verse 13: 'I can do everything through Him who gives me strength.' We cannot rise above the circumstances of life on our own. But the Lord is near and His Holy Spirit is His presence with us and is His help for us, therefore we can do

77

all things through Him. 'For I can do everything with the help of Christ, who gives me the strength I need' (New Living Translation).

If we trust God like this, if we depend on His providential care and His presence and power to help us, joy will increase. And as joy increases in our life, it will increase in others also.

True spirituality then means that *Jesus is our joy*. True spirituality is God-centred. It is Jesus-focused. It is cross appreciating. It is Spirit helped. It is Bible fed and nourished. It is service motivated. It is ever hopeful about the future because heaven is our home. It is trusting and it is joyful because of God's love and providential concern for us.

Joy is our birthright and true spirituality is to live in the joy of our relationship with Christ. May we by God's grace enter into and develop that relationship day by day, and discover the source of unceasing joy.

Let Paul have the final word:

'And this same God who takes care of me will supply all your needs from His glorious riches, which have been given to us in Christ Jesus. Now glory be to God our Father for ever and ever. Amen' (4:19, 20, New Living Translation).

BIBLIOGRAPHY

F. F. Bruce, *Philippians,* New International Biblical Commentary, Hendrickson.

Gordon Fee, *Paul's letter to the Philippians*, NICNT, Eerdmans.

Sinclair B. Ferguson, *Let's Study Philippians*, Banner of Truth.

John Gwyn-Thomas, *Rejoice Always* (Studies in Philippians 4), Banner of Truth.

William Lane, *Philippians*, Scripture Union.

Alister E. McGrath, *Evangelical Spirituality*, St. Antholin's Lecture.

Alec Motyer, *The Message of Philippians*, The Bible Speaks Today, IVP.

J. I. Packer, *An Anglican to Remember. William Perkins: Puritan Popularizer*, St. Antholin's Lecture.

REFERENCES

1. Alister E McGrath. 'Evangelical Spirituality', St. Antholin's Lectureship Charity Lecture, 1993.
2. C.S. Lewis, *The Problem of Pain*, p.81.
3. See also St Augustine: 'Whence has water so great an efficacy as in touching the body to cleanse the soul, save by the operation of the Word; and that *not because it is uttered, but because it is believed?*' Tract. LXXX, on the Gospel of John (italics mine).
4. William Lane, *Scripture Union Bible Study Books*, p.38.
5. Alec Motyer, *Message of Philippians* (*Bible Speaks Today*) p.166.

6. William Lane, *Scripture Union Bible Study Books*, 1969, 'Philippians', p.40.

7. Gordon Fee, *Philippians*, 1995, Eerdmans, p.334.

8. C. H. Spurgeon, *Morning and Evening Daily Readings*, Christian Focus Publications.

9. *Through the Year with J. I. Packer* (Hodder), p.306.

10. F. F. Bruce, *Philippians*, NIBC, Hendrickson, 1989.

11. Motyer, p.108.

12. Ward Gasque/R. Martin, *Apostolic History and the Gospel, Paternoster*, 1970..

13. Motyer, p.113.

14. Graham Kendrick, 1983, *Thank You Music*.

15. Motyer,

16. Bruce Ballinger, Lorenz Publishing Co/MCA Publishing Co and Copycare.

17. Joni Eareckson Tada, *Heaven*, (Marshall Pickering).

18. John Gwyn-Thomas, *Rejoice Always*, Banner of Truth, p.55.

19. John Gwyn-Thomas, *Rejoice Always,* p.51.

20. St. Antholin's Lecture. 'An Anglican to Remember', *William Perkins: Puritan Popularizer* by J. I. Packer, p.13.

21. Motyer, p.219.

22. John Gwyn-Thomas, p.97.